Royal

Biographies
Volume 9

William and Kate

2 Books in 1

Katy Holborn and Michael
Woodford

Table of Contents

Prince William

A Prince William Biography

Katy Holborn

Prince William

A Spotlight on the 'Reluctant' Royal

Even before Prince William was born, the eyes of the world were already trained firmly in his direction.

His mother, Diana, was a shy, stunning beauty who had captured the heart of the heir to the British throne. The fresh-faced aristocrat worked as a kindergarten assistant and was only 19 years old when they fell in love – or, in Prince Charles' infamous words after their engagement was announced, *"Whatever 'in love' means."* Her romance with Charles would propel her into an entirely different life from the quieter one she knew as Lady Diana Spencer. The shy English rose was suddenly cast in a role few people in the world are really equipped for – that of leading lady in a fairy tale everyone desperately wanted to end in happily ever after.

There was a picture-perfect wedding in July 1981 and shortly after, in November of the same year, a joyful announcement that a child was on the way. She was only 20 years old at the time, already navigating the minefield of modern royalty meshed with modern celebrity, treading the line between the public and the private.

As mother to a child slated for the throne of a powerful country, it was of no surprise that everyone was paying close attention to the pregnant princess. But Diana stoked interest on her own merits too. With her beauty and quiet charisma, coupled with a warmth and openness unprecedented in the royal family, the public simply couldn't get enough of her. This fixation would only intensify with her pregnancy. Later biographies and interviews of the princess would reveal her feelings about the pressures of carrying a royal child – as if the world was watching her stomach. As if she was being monitored daily. As if the whole country was with her in labor…

In many ways, she was right. Fixations with the royal baby bump and the pressures of carrying a child in line to the throne were not new of course, but hers was a different time. The 1980s presented economic uncertainty, cultural shifts and heady changes for the British people. There was far less deference to the monarchy. There was greater freedom of speech. The iconic punk band, the Sex Pistols, for example, had released their provocative single, *God Save the Queen* just a few years prior in 1977. With lyrics like *"She's not a human being"* and *"There's no future,"* it was brash, disillusioned, anti-establishment – and a veritable hit that would be remembered even now, not only as one of the greatest songs of all time and for its seminal part in shaping Rock and Roll, but also for capturing a sense of the era. Part of that times was characterized by a monarchy that seemed crippled by rigid formality, out of touch, and somewhat detached from the tougher realities faced by most of the country.

But then came Charles and Diana's fairy tale, and in Diana, the arrival onto the scene of a modern princess who was forging her way beneath the limelight – and into people's hearts. When she became pregnant, she had also taken on a symbolic relevance, as a writer for the *New York Times* would eventually put it; her pregnancy was a link to the past and a promise for the future. A pregnant princess, it seemed, was a literal embodiment of a sense of continuity for the monarchy.

Even before Prince William was born, therefore, he was already carrying the hopes of his people on his shoulders. He already had burdens and faced high expectations.

The 1980s was also an age of technology, information, celebrity, and consumerism. There was insatiable public demand for information on and photographs of the royal family and consequently, intense competition from press outlets. This, in turn, would foster relentless media attention that would only deepen for the Royals over time. That attention would never leave them, and in particular, would hound Diana, the People's Princess, even unto death.

Princess Diana suffered under that media scrutiny brutally. Later, Prince William would reveal in a candid documentary, *Diana: Our Mother*, how crying over press intrusion was a regular occurrence for the Princess, who had been chased, blocked and even spat on by the press that constantly hounded her. Intense though it may have been for Princess Diana, however, she was in the public eye mainly after being romantically linked to Prince Charles. She had, in a sense, 19 years of relative freedom before that. Their son Prince William, on the other hand, would be subject to the glare of cameras all his life.

He was a baby in his mom's belly when
photos of Princess Diana in Barbados,
wearing a bikini while pregnant, made
worldwide headlines when they came out in
1982. The press would be there on Prince
William's first day of life too, camping
outside the hospital where he was born, well
placed to catch a photo of him when he was
presented to the world as a baby covered in a
plush white blanket in his mother's arms.
There would be photos of him growing up,
dressed for school, trying to live a normal
life while caught between feuding parents.
There would be unforgettable, heartbreaking
images of him walking behind his mother's
casket in her funeral procession. She was
famously killed in a car crash partially
attributed to a gaggle of paparazzi
photographers who had all but chased her to

death. There would be revealing photographs of his wife, Katherine the Duchess of Cambridge, while sunbathing in private on vacation. Racy photos of his brother, Prince Harry, enjoying a wild night out with friends in Las Vegas would also come out. There would be cunning means of acquiring photos of Prince William's children too, including actions that could be considered stalking and allegedly, the use of other children to bait the youngest royals into a playful photo op.

Royals of any age have always led interesting lives, and people have always been interested in knowing all about them. Our history books, for instance, are bursting with anecdotes of the eccentricities and misbehavior, of the trials, triumphs, and tragedies, of many royal figures long before this generation. But the public's current access to information, as well as its sense of entitlement to receiving them, is unprecedented.

Prince William's mother, Diana, stepped into the limelight upon her romance with Prince Charles. The royals before them were able to have more private lives, due to limited technology and more public deference to the monarchy. Now, there are telephoto lenses enhancing the reach of cameras. Data can be hacked and leaked, phones can be tapped and conversations recorded. Everyone has a smartphone with camera and video. Everyone has become a potential paparazzi.

Based on his family history, it shouldn't come as a surprise to anyone if Prince William had a bit of a bone to pick with the press (as he is accused of having). But as modern royals with limited actual power in government, the family also has an understanding of their symbolic roles; and part of symbolism is imagery and public access to their lives. They know they have to work with the media. In this way, the family has learned, and is continuing to learn, how to live with and leverage the power of the press to be able to do their work and pursue their advocacies.

Undoubtedly, many more authorized and unauthorized photos and information are still in the cards for the royal family in the future. But they're making compromises too, like agreeing to more public events in exchange for more respect for their private moments. They've also made surprising and very modern strides forward, for example in announcing the Duke and Duchess of Cambridge's third pregnancy via the social media platform, Twitter and having official social media accounts. Though the royals' social media presence is externally managed, very proper and sometimes impersonal, it is still a sign of this family's constant ability to adjust and move with the times to stay relevant. The Royal Family has an account, as does Prince Charles and second wife the Duchess of Cornwall via Clarence House. And for inquiring minds - yes, they all use hashtags!

By the time Prince William takes the crown as King, we will have a man on the throne with unparalleled amounts of documentation on his life, available on all forms of media. There will be photos and videos, press releases, magazine articles, books, documentaries, movies and TV shows, and 140-character statements, even. He will certainly be amongst the most watched royals of all time.

We don't have to wonder about the accuracy of royal portraits painted by master artists, we have photos of Prince William aplenty, in every age. We don't have to dig up and decipher old letters and wonder about salacious love affairs; "William + Ex-girlfriends" are but a few clicks away on a search engine. We have so much information that we can even find the former relationships of his wife, and the former relationships of their former relationships. When it comes to Prince William, we simply won't have to dig so deep or scratch our heads in too much mystery. If anything, we have more information than we know what to do with.

True to the information age Prince William lives in and will one day reign in, the problem in understanding the life of a royal so deeply entrenched in the public sphere, isn't so much that we have limited information, but what, from all the data that is out there, can be counted as relevant information?

In one of Prince William's most famous photographs growing up, we see him in an apron and we know he was cooking chicken paella at Eton. Of the famed 90s girl pop group, The Spice Girls, we know he may have had a poster of "Baby Spice" Emma Bunton on his walls. He is apparently bad at video games, calling himself *"enthusiastic but quite useless*" as a gamer. And speaking of gaming... he was interested in acquiring a Playstation, but needed to figure out how his wife felt about it first.

These are just random trivia that show we know so much and see so much of the young royal who will one day be King. But what can we really make of what we've seen? We think we have an idea of him as a son, as a husband, as a father. But what is important of all the information that is out there? What are the key events that have shaped his life, and how might he be as a monarch? Is he really, as some in the press have alleged, a "reluctant royal" who would rather have a quiet life in the country? Could he be "work-shy" with light hours and limited loads, especially compared to his grandparents, Queen Elizabeth and Prince Philip, who have stayed in grueling public service well into their 90s? Is he really restrictive of press freedom? How will he be working alongside the government, while maintaining political neutrality as royals are expected to be?

Of all the quantity of information that we have on Prince William, what is really worth knowing about the man who is second in line to the throne?

Charles and Diana's Son

On the 21st of June, 1982, a boy, the eldest child of Princess Diana and Prince Charles of Wales, was born. Prince William Arthur Philip Louis, is second-in-line to a throne over 1,000 years old. He has a rich life ahead of him, but on the morning that he was first presented to the public, on the steps of London's St. Mary's Hospital very shortly after his birth, the 7-pound, 1 and ½ ounce boy was just a little blue-eyed baby in a blanket, in the arms of his parents.

His father, the reserved Prince Charles, was 33-years old and his mother, the shy Diana, was 20. They were young and beautiful and looked delighted. They married just a little over a year earlier in July, in a lavish ceremony viewed by millions of people all over the world. It was just like a fairytale, and the birth of their child, a son and an heir to the throne, was just one more piece in the picture-perfect puzzle of the happily ever after everyone was craving. Over the years, it would become painfully clear to all that behind the scenes, that was not at all the case. By some accounts, even the early years of their marriage and the duration of Diana's pregnancy were far from idyllic.

Even before Prince William was born, he would already be experiencing the tumult of his parents' stormy relationship. In a candid conversation revealed later by the National Geographic in a documentary titled *Diana: In Her Own Words*, a despondent Princess shared how she had once been so unhappy that she threw herself down a flight of stairs while pregnant. It was a cry for help and it would not be her last one along the course of her troubled existence behind the gilded walls of her palace life.

In this way and in many others, there would be no discussion of the kind of man William is, without first looking at the life of his parents.

A "Crowded" Marriage

Lady Diana Spencer, as daughter of Earl Spencer, had a privileged life. It was plagued by the marital woes of her own family, but she was a beautiful woman with a pedigree, and moved in the rarified circles of the royal family. Her older sister Sarah had even caught the eye of Charles, the Prince of

Wales, and they dated for a time. While that relationship ultimately came to nothing, Diana too would catch the reserved royal's attention. He was in his early thirties and she was 19 when they began a relationship in 1980.

The young woman fell under heavy media scrutiny, and by some accounts, Prince Charles' father, the royal consort Prince Philip, would write to his son and encourage him to either settle down with Diana or to let her go, out of consideration for her reputation. Prince Charles, who may have interpreted the missive as a command, proposed to Diana and the couple would marry shortly after her 20th birthday in July 1981. Later reports would reveal they both entertained reservations before taking that dive into marriage – after all, they did reportedly go on just 12 dates before getting engaged - but the ceremony itself was stunning and captured the imagination of the world.

Unfortunately, it was all a collective fantasy that would unravel equally publicly.

Diana gave birth to William a year after their wedding, in 1982. William's younger brother, Prince Henry Charles Albert David, would follow two years later in September 1984. Even then, however, it seemed the relationship between their parents was crumbling. Charles was reportedly not enthusiastic about the redheaded baby boy, and Diana believed her husband had already resumed a relationship with his long-time love (and now current wife, the Duchess of Cornwall), Camilla. Things would only deteriorate from there, in spite of everyone's desire to see the marriage work, including efforts from Prince Charles' parents, Queen Elizabeth II and Prince Philip, at an intervention.

By mid-1992, biographer Andrew Morton's seminal *Diana: Her True Story - in Her Own Words*, was released, and it was apparent to many that the Princess had actively participated in its writing. It is searing and authoritative. The dirty laundry was out, and it wouldn't be the last to be aired publicly. Later the same year, the so-called "Squidgygate tapes" were unleashed to the world… a conversation between the Princess, nicknamed "Squidgy" by her friend and alleged lover, James Gilbey, and the man himself, who would say it several times throughout the record. This was followed by an official visit to South Korea, where the dynamics of the relationship was watched closely – from their glum expressions to hostile body language - and deemed doomed. The official announcement of their separation would follow shortly after their return home.

Morton's book became a huge bestseller, and its subject, Princess Diana, appeared to the public as a sympathetic, tortured figure. A vilified Prince Charles did not help himself when a work-related TV documentary for the Prince's Trust that aired in 1994, eventually turned into a more personal interview, with a revelation on adultery when his relationship with Diana deteriorated. Though damaging, this is a far less shocking affair than the "Camillagate" tapes leaked earlier, in which recorded phone conversations would reveal the Prince reportedly joked about wishing to be his lover's tampon.

But Diana was not done with her own revelations. In November 1995, she fired back with a tell-all interview before journalist Martin Bashir of the BBC. The Panorama Interview, as it would eventually be known, was unflinching, brutal and unforgettable. She admitted to infidelity, shared her struggles with mental issues, and had said the now-iconic, *"There were three of us in this marriage, so it was a bit crowded."* Some royal watchers have even called the consequent fallout as the worst crisis to hit the monarchy since Edward VIII's abdication in the 1930s, when the then-King fell in love with American divorcee Wallis Simpson but could not find family, political or public support to marry her.

By 1995 even Queen Elizabeth II had reportedly had enough of the tumultuous relationship – writing to Charles and Diana separately about seeking a divorce.

The year 1996 would see the divorce become final and Diana, though stripped of her styling as "Her Royal Highness," was permitted to continue residing at an apartment in Kensington Palace, and was reportedly given a handsome lump sum settlement of $22.5 million along with an annual $600,000 for her office. She had access to family assets like the jet and state apartments at St. James's Palace, and was even allowed to keep most of the jewelry from the marriage. As a member of the royal family and mother to the princes, she was still welcome to some state and public events. Most importantly, she and Charles had equal access to Princes William and Harry, who were at the time only 14 and 11 years of age, with whom they shared precious time when the boys were not in boarding school.

After the divorce, Princess Diana continued with her advocacies, most memorably walking through a minefield in Angola in January 1997, as part of the Red Cross' fight against the use of landmines. It was one more iconic image for a woman who had a lifetime of making them; she looked fearless and determined. Her courage and hard work are some of the reasons why she was so beloved and continues to be sorely missed, as that same year would put an end to her too-short life. By the end of August 1997, she was dead, killed in a tragic car accident in Paris with her new boyfriend, Dodi Fayed. Their intoxicated driver was trying to flee paparazzi.

Prince Charles, along with Diana's sisters, Sarah and Jane, retrieved her body from Paris and brought her back home, where a funeral fit for a royal and a beloved public figure was held before she was finally laid to rest in her family's storied Althorp estate. Her brother Earl Spencer, flanked by her two loving sons and they in turn flanked by their father Prince Charles and grandfather Prince Philip, famously walked behind her casket in the funeral procession. It was a heartbreaking sight.

As of this writing, Prince William is 35 years old, a few weeks shy of his 36th birthday, the age of his mother when she died. He is by now, alive for longer than he had his mum, who passed away when he was only 15. There is a lot of his life after Diana, but she would always be a part of it. From the obvious – like how he and his brother speak of her lovingly and openly and manage her public memory, and how the two princes made sure their respective fiancées would carry pieces of her jewelry – to the subtle but more fundamental, like how they continue her advocacies, champion open conversations on mental health issues, and how in particular, Prince William relates warily with the press and raises his family in a very hands-on way.

Prince William's Early Years

All of these would come later of course, as the two princes grew beneath the watchful eyes of the public as more or less well-adjusted and self-possessed young men. But during the time of their parents' tumultuous relationship, Prince William and Prince Harry struggled as many kids from broken families would have struggled – except magnified to the nth degree.

What other child, after all, would need to have a conversation with their mother about the restoration of a royal title? It will be recalled that part of the divorce entailed the stripping of Diana's "HRH." She was still "Diana, Princess of Wales," but the removal of "Her Royal Highness" – allegedly insisted upon by her ex-husband – meant she was required to curtsy to whoever still had the honorific, including her own sons. If rumors hold true, a young Prince William had once told her he would give her back the title when he became king.

The tumultuous years of Charles and Diana's trying relationship could not have been easy on their children, especially as William and Harry got older and became more exposed to it. After all, they had to juggle the concerns of normal children, like school and sports, on top of having to live up to the expectations foisted on them by their positions, growing up before the eyes of the world, and dealing with their family problems.

Prince William was a student at Mrs. Mynor's Nursery School in London from 1985 to 1987, and then at Weatherby School in Kensington from 1987-1990. At age 8, he would be sent to boarding school at Ludgrove Preparatory School, an institution which was at the time, almost 100 years old and previously attended by other aristocrats. He had bodyguards here, but was otherwise like the other kids in that he was to share a dorm room with other boys, use a communal bathroom, and keep to a schedule for meals, classes, prayers, and bedtime. Phone calls home were not allowed, and weekends spent outside campus were limited – tough restrictions for a boy of 8, even if he weren't His Royal Highness Prince William of Wales! The comprehensive education (covering a wide range of subjects including Art and French alongside Carpentry) came with trappings too though, with access to sports facilities including a pool and a nine-hole golf course.

Being away from school was tough, but in some ways, it offered stability as his parents' relationship deteriorated. Prince William stayed in Ludgrove from 1990 to 1995 – which were years of rapid decline for the marriage of Charles and Diana. In Ludgrove though, he had structure and a determined set of protectors, including some who reportedly shielded him from press coverage of his breaking family by keeping him away from the papers.

It was harder to protect him when he left Ludgrove for another storied institution, Eton College. It was hard enough for any new boy adjusting to a new and prestigious school, but Prince William also had to deal with his parents' scandalous relationship plastered across the front pages of the nation's papers. His years at Eton, from 1995 to 2000, would see some tough years for the royal family and especially for himself. Scandal after scandal included an alleged romance between his mother and rugby captain Will Carling, followed by Diana's Panorama interview in 1995. This was only on his first term. The Panorama interview was reportedly watched by the young Prince in the study of his housemaster and affected him deeply; as it would any child to hear their parents speak ill of each other or make their family problems known to others. But by 1996 there was the divorce and after that, his mother's shocking death in 1997.

It wasn't easy being Charles and Diana's son, but William's parents had their own shortcomings as individuals, apart from their conflicts with each other. Prince Charles, for example, was widely criticized for being an absentee parent in their earlier years, most notably after William had an accident in Ludgrove that necessitated a surgery to the head. Diana, for her part, while clearly a loving and passionate mother, suffered from mental issues that reportedly exposed her children to spells of tears, hysterics, and extreme moods. With their parents' busy schedules, the princes also spent much of their time with household staff, like their nannies. A particularly devoted one, Barbara Barnes, would make a lasting impression on William.

He called her "Baba" and she was a comfort to the rambunctious young royal, reading to him, sharing meals and giving him hugs.

Diana was rumored to be uncomfortable or even jealous of Barbara, who would eventually be let go for mysterious reasons. She would always be in William's heart, however, and she even got a coveted invitation to the Prince's wedding to Catherine Middleton 25 years later.

How any young man can come out of all the public and private drama with his sanity intact is a marvel. But to come out having excelled in school must be no less than a miracle. He was well-liked, excelled in sports and also good in academics. When Prince William left Eton in 2000, he was awarded A, B and C grades in his A-levels, Geography, History of Art and Biology, respectively. These, along with 10 GCSEs of eight As and two Bs, were said to put him amongst the brightest of the royal family.His schooling achievements showed promise of an intelligent future King. But at that time, his grades were great for another reason – they were good enough to secure him a spot at prestigious St. Andrew's University. There, he would be put in the path of a beautiful young woman who would forever change his life – that of Catherine Middleton, his future wife.

Prince William in Love

On the rugged shores of Scotland sits an intimate, medieval town called St. Andrews. Downtown is a simple affair of a few short streets and a Cathedral, but its environs are scenic and dramatic, with coastal views of jagged cliffs and crashing seas, golf courses, beaches, and centuries-old structures. There are picturesque streets and quaint shops, but also mansions and spired buildings. The town is home to a prestigious educational institution, St. Andrews University, that is considered one of the best not only in the United Kingdom but also in the world. Founded in 1413, it is the first Scottish university, but it also holds a more endearing distinction – it must be a wonderful place to fall in love.

The town is intimate and the student life diverse and thriving. In this coastal town, urban distractions are a distant reality (including paparazzi!). Friendships are formed and unique, unforgettable memories are made. If some estimates are to be believed, one in ten of its students marries a person they encountered while studying. Just ask, for example, the royal couple, Prince William and his wife, Duchess Catherine.

Before Kate

A man in line to inherit the British throne would have had his pick of the ladies even if he weren't as handsome or as personable as Prince William. But the son of Prince Charles and Princess Diana has a list of conquests that is both relatively short and generally has little-verified information.

Jessica "Jecca" Craig, a stunning, strong-willed brunette, is said to have captured the Prince's heart when they were teenagers. The Craigs moved in fancy environmentalist circles, and her father, Ian Craig, who owned a ranch in Kenya, was good friends with the late brother of Prince Charles' beloved Camilla. They were family friends, and Prince William spent some time at the family's Kenyan ranch during his gap year. Whether or not they really dated or for how seriously is unverified. What is apparent is that they remain friendly, and William would go on to attend her brother's wedding in 2008, she would be a presence in his and Kate's in 2011, they set tongues wagging when they hunted wild boar and stag with friends in Spain in 2014, and he flew all the way from the UK to attend Jecca's own wedding in Kenya in 2016.

Prince William and childhood friend Rose Farquhar, daughter of former Master of the Beaufort Hunt, Captain Ian Farquhar, dated briefly in the year 2000. The aspiring singer and actress would later on appear in TV talent shows like *How Do You Solve a Problem Like Maria?*, a 2006 search for an actress to play Maria in *The Sound of Music* on West End; and singing competition, *The Voice* in 2016. Her resume also includes the pursuit of her craft at the prestigious Lee Strasberg Institute in New York. There are no publicly available details on this failed romance, but one of the things many royal watchers can agree on, is that Ms. Farquhar has similar looks to the woman Prince William would eventually marry.

Arabella Musgrave, whom the Prince had also known since they were little, really caught his eye in the summer of 2001, just before he headed for St. Andrew's. They danced and drank and had a passionate romance that cooled down as Prince William had to leave for university. For a time, it was reported that they saw each other whenever he returned. As part of the "Glosse Posse-" close friends of the Prince from Gloucestershire - the glamorous PR exec of Gucci would be in attendance at the Prince's wedding to Catherine Middleton in 2011.

The Prince's first semester at St. Andrews saw him dating Carley Massy-Birch, a self-confessed country bumpkin. It was a trait that appealed to the Prince, who had a love for the countryside. It probably did not hurt that Carley had what many remember to be a legendary derrière. They had a short-lived romance that allegedly ended due to the Prince's continued links with Arabella Musgrave. The relationship was so low-key it would not be known publicly until years after they graduated.

Olivia Hunt was also early in capturing Prince William's heart while he was at St. Andrew's, but she was quickly out of the picture when Kate Middleton came sashaying down the runway at a charity fashion show and made an impression on the Prince in her see-through dress. Olivia, a writer, reportedly remains friends with the couple and they have even gone skiing together. They move in the same circles and when she married one of the UK's "hottest" barristers, Nicholas Wilkinson, in 2016, Prince Harry and a number of their common friends were in attendance. She also attended Pippa Middleton's wedding in 2017.

The blue-blooded actress, heiress, and socialite, Isabella Calthorpe, has an impressive pedigree via parents John Anstruther-Gough-Calthorpe and Lady Mary-Gaye Georgiana Lorna Curzon. She could have been a more traditional match for Prince William… even if one didn't see the slight resemblance she had with the Prince's stunning mother, Diana. She and the Prince reportedly met at a dinner party in 2001 and chatted the night away at a ball in 2004 or 2005, but wouldn't be seriously linked to each other until William and Kate's brief separation later. The romance wouldn't get very far – the Prince's affections were not returned, if accounts are true! - and Isabella eventually married billionaire Sir Richard Branson's son, Sam, in 2013.

The above list shows a friend who might have been more, puppy love, the passionate summer romance, the quiet country secret, the one the Prince let go, and the one who would do the same to him. But as one of the world's most eligible bachelors, Prince William would be romantically linked with other women to varying degrees. There's Davina Duckworth-Chad, who joined him, his friends and family in an Aegean cruise in 1999. Rumors of flirtations and brief relationships would be in the news too, such as with equestrienne Rosie van Cutsem and security consultant Natalie Hicks-Lobbecke. There would be petite blonde Tess Shepherd too, with whom the Prince reportedly shared a drunken, dancefloor embrace at London hotspot Boujis.

But for all of these women's bloodlines, impressive names and royal connections, the Prince's heart would eventually be claimed by his university roommate, Kate Middleton – daughter of former airline employees turned party supply millionaires, and whose mother's side was in the working class, including a store clerk, builders, laborers and coal miners. "Commoner Kate," sneered some. "New Money," said others. But by her grace and poise, she would make her own way forward as one-half of the world's most watched and beloved couples.

Catherine Middleton

Catherine Elizabeth Middleton is the eldest of Michael and Carole Middleton's three children. She was born on the 9th of January, 1982, in Reading, Berkshire, England. At the time of her birth, her parents were airline employees. When she was two years old, the family moved to Amman, Jordan, where they lived for two and a half years as her father worked. She attended nursery school there when she turned three. They returned to Berkshire in 1986, and soon afterwards she enrolled at co-educational St. Andrew's School in Pangbourne.

The family would undergo a major change in 1987, when her parents founded Party Pieces, a mail order company supplying party paraphernalia. The company's success would turn the couple into multi-millionaires, with recent estimates pegging a value of $50 million on the thriving business. Kate and her younger siblings, Pippa (born in 1984) and James (born in 1987), would consequently have a comfortable life and excellent opportunities in schooling.

Kate was a student at St. Andrew's School until 1995, and she would later describe her time there as amongst the happiest years of her life. She discovered a love and talent for sport here, and by one of her teacher's accounts, held a long-standing record at the high jump that would only be broken after 20 years. One of the most famous stories to come out about Kate Middleton during her time in St. Andrew's School is that she was involved in public speaking and drama. A video surfaced of her as a young girl in a school play, portraying a character who is told by a fortune teller that she would marry a prince – which as the world knows, would one day come true!

After the happy time she spent at St. Andrew's School, she would get a bit of a shock at the next place she enrolled in. Kate spent a brief time at all-girls school Downe House, where she reportedly was either a victim of intense bullying or was someone who simply did not find it the right fit. Either way, she stayed all of two terms before being moved away at age 14. Rumors of her ever having been bullied were never confirmed, but she gave royal watchers something to read into when she and Prince William included the charity, Beatbullying, in a list of charities wedding guests and other well-wishers could donate to in lieu of gifts to them on their special day. Even after their marriage, she and Prince William would continue to be an advocate for victims of bullying.

Following her rough time at Downe House, she attended co-educational Marlborough College in Wiltshire, where she remained until the year 2000. It's a prestigious institution too, counting Princess Eugenie as one of its alumni. While there, Kate showed athletic prowess and participated in sports like hockey, netball, and tennis. She also studied A-level Chemistry, Biology and Art. She would eventually pass 11 GCSEs and 3 A-level exams, marks that would allow her into a prestigious institution like St. Andrew's University in Scotland, where she would eventually find her Prince Charming.

From Friend to Future Queen

Before enrolling at St. Andrew's University in Scotland, Kate Middleton had a stimulating gap year, with stints in the British Institute in Florence and spending time in Chile with British charity Raleigh International, among other pursuits. Prince William had his own gap year adventures. He spent time in Kenya (and time getting closer to Jecca Craig, if rumors are to be believed), and was also in Latin America with Raleigh International. His travels and volunteer work had him doing a variety of tasks, including building a playground in Chile, painting homes, and milking cows on an English farm. His busy schedule wouldn't let his social life suffer, however; he'd reportedly had time to date Arabella Musgrave before heading off to university.

Prince William and Catherine Middleton missed each other in Chile only by a few weeks. They were tossed in different places in the world and cavorting with different people, but inevitably, their paths were slowly winding their way toward each other.

St. Andrew's University, as had been previously described, seems like a great place to live, learn and fall in love. Prince William's time there would give him unprecedented freedom to do just these things, especially because the small town was not only far from the hustle, bustle and easy press access of a big city, but arrangements were also made with the media to generally have respect for the young prince's privacy during his education. This allowed the young prince a lot of space for pursuing as much of a "normal life" as a man of his stature could ever hope to have. Over his time there, the small town, with its population of less than 20,000 people, generally left him alone to do ordinary things like walking in the streets or shopping at the grocery store.

Prince William's schooling in St. Andrew's is a break from royal tradition; 150 years of history would see royal families in either Oxford or Cambridge, including William's father Charles, uncle Edward, and great-grandfather King George VI. Though it was lovely at St. Andrew's and he found friends (and dates like the quiet suppers he is said to have shared with Carley Massy-Birch) fairly easily, the university he ultimately chose for himself was 50 miles up from Edinburgh and could be confining and stark to someone used to an entirely different life. William was a long way from home and missed his friends, the London nightlife, and, if reports are to be believed, the company of Arabella Musgrave, too. He was homesick, on top of allegedly finding the coursework at St. Andrew's challenging. The Prince discussed his misgivings with his understanding father, Prince Charles, and the school worked with them to help adjust. From his art history major he switched to Geography, and eventually settled in much better.

His friendships would play no small part in that, including a kinship he found with athletic, pretty and shy Kate Middleton, whom he would often run into at St. Salvator's, one of the residence halls in the university. She shared his first major, and though he would eventually deviate from this, they had many other similar interests and plenty of opportunities to know each other better. They shared healthy meals at the dining hall with their other friends, and enjoyed sports like swimming and skiing.

Other than meeting in school, and details of the shy future duchess blushing and 'scuttling off,' the precise circumstances of their meeting are unknown. A biography of Kate, citing sources from her time in Marlborough, would later claim the couple were actually introduced by common friends earlier than when they were at St. Andrew's. While that information is not confirmed, some quarters have pointed out how Kate made a surprising shift from her original plans of enrolling at Edinburgh University, said to be her first choice, to deciding on St. Andrew's. The information fits into the narrative pushed by some people that

Catherine Middleton is more calculating than she would have the public believe, but this is just one mystery the rest of us would simply have to live with, at least for now.

At any rate, there are relatively few secrets between this couple and the public, and much more is known about how their love story unfolded after that fateful first meeting (whenever or wherever that might have actually been).

Prince William kept a low-key and some might even say, a rather boring life in St. Andrews. He would swim and go cycling, and made the occasional appearance at the student union to play pool. He spent time with his friends and immersed in school activities, one of which would prove a turning point in his life. It was March 2002, and he wouldn't be looking at his friend Kate Middleton the same way again.

Kate was a known beauty, deemed amongst the prettiest in "Sally's," as their St. Salvator's residence is known. She and William had been friends for some time, but on one evening in March 2002, at the yearly Don't Walk fashion show for charity, she took the runway in black underwear beneath a see-through dress. The Prince was in the front row and he, like everyone else, knew she looked "hot."

A witness who was present at a post-show after-party would later claim that the Prince made a move that very night. He appeared to have leaned in for a kiss, which was dodged cleanly by the woman who would one day be his wife and Duchess. She was said to be dating someone else at the time, a fourth-year student named Rupert Finch. She may have also wanted to play it cool, and give an otherwise privileged prince a little bit more to work for.

Either way, whether or not Kate Middleton had intended to do so, it seemed as if she had snagged herself a Prince.

At the beginning of Prince William's second year, in 2002, he moved out of the campus residence halls in favor of living in an apartment with his friends. He roomed in with Kate and their pals, Olivia Bleasdale and his fellow former Etonian, Fergus Boyd.

Moving into the centrally-located 13a Hope Street offered Prince William a shot at a normal college life. They paid rent. They cleaned and shopped for groceries at the local Tesco, and they hosted dinner parties. Perfectly ordinary - except of course, with bomb-proof doors, bullet-proof windows, and a complex laser security system. Absolutely normal too, for a student like him to find and nurture a university love – except of course, that he and Kate had to keep their growing relationship a closely guarded secret.

It wouldn't last for very long and soon, their secret became an "open secret" in the university. In a bid for more privacy, the couple moved away from the city center to Balgove House, a property owned by the prince's distant cousin, Henry Cheape. The four-bedroom cottage sat on a private estate that was large enough to have outbuildings that could house the Prince's security officers, as well as to have sprawling, walled grounds that allowed the couple to enjoy picnics and long, romantic walks.

But the secret that became an open secret would cease to be a secret of any kind by the first quarter of 2004, during a ski trip to the Klosters in Switzerland. Photos of William and Kate were splashed across the papers, visual confirmation of the rumors long circulating that the Prince was in a serious relationship. The Prince had a girlfriend, and the scoop was too delicious for the press to seriously keep to the agreement they had with the Palace regarding the Prince's privacy while at university. Suddenly everyone wanted to know about Kate.

Prince William was aware of what dating him could mean for a girl. In an interview, he talked about how his dating someone could put that person in an awkward situation, and he was right. Kate Middleton would hold that awkward position for a long time, but it was one of the ways that she shined. She was polite and discreet, and had a family who was just as careful. She kept a cool head and kept herself grounded, even as attention on their relationship intensified.

As a modern couple of extraordinary means, they had a lot of opportunities to get to know each other better outside of university too. Getaways included Kate accompanying William to Balmoral, Highgrove, and Sandringham for hunting seasons, sometimes with friends and other times with Kate's siblings, Pippa and James. Aside from hunting, they enjoyed activities like cooking, taking long walks in the moors or just enjoying being together before a roaring log fire.

But the Prince seemed to need more than quiet country sojourns in his life as an in-demand young royal. He had a rather outgoing group of friends too, and enjoyed the occasional gregarious activity. By mid-2004 he was reportedly getting restless in St. Andrew's, and his relationship with Kate was experiencing some strain. Finals were coming too and soon after that, graduation and the end of the quiet life they've crafted in the small town that was home for their years of studying. Questions remained on how the couple would navigate life outside of university, moving forward.

Some time apart seemed to be in order to clarify things. William, along with some friends, planned an all-boys sailing vacation to Greece. Among these friends were the controversial but loyal Guy Pelly, whom Kate allegedly did not completely approve of (he would eventually be a valued ally, and was close enough to the couple to be a rumored godparent to their son, Prince George). She wouldn't be alone in this assessment, if she did think it of him at the time. Mr. Pelly, whom the press have called a party animal and was known as the "court jester" of their illustrious group, seemed to have a talent for fun. He ran some of London's hottest nightclubs, a talent he may have honed when he, along with the Princes William and Harry, allegedly had wild, private, drunken get-togethers with their friends. During William's planned Greek holiday, Kate spent part of the summer with her family in Berkshire and part of it in France, where she reportedly confided to friends of their relationship issues. William, if rumors are to be believed, wasn't just longing for his old social whirlwind, he was also somewhat interested in other women, perhaps Jecca Craig and/or Isabella Calthorpe.

It was still Kate, however, who would be spending time with William's family during Prince Charles' birthday, and on the holiday to Klosters just before Prince Charles married his beloved Camilla in a civil ceremony. And when the young couple finally graduated from St. Andrew's University in 2005, it was still Kate that William would spend his free time with before setting off for the Royal Military Academy at Sandhurst.

By 2006, they would be photographed kissing in public for the first time, again while on a skiing holiday. As they went on more travels and public events, and would be seen together when William wasn't away in training, the seriousness of the relationship was clear to many. There was talk of the couple going down the aisle soon – but not quite, from William's mouth.

Will They or Won't They?

One of Kate Middleton's most important public appearances before their marriage was when she and her parents, who had also become close to the Prince, were invited to attend William's 2006 graduation ceremony at Sandhurst. Quite an honor, considering the Prince had also invited his grandmother the Queen, and his dad Prince Charles and wife Camilla, the Duchess of Cornwall. The bets were on – a royal engagement must be in the cards, and soon.

In the meantime, Kate Middleton suffered the rigors of being a public persona, with none of the perks and only the barest of protections. She was given advice on how to handle the media, had some support from a press team, and the occasional protection officer. She handled things well even when she was swamped by photographers, and was always a cool customer with great, accessible style. If rumors are to be believed, sometimes she was even more cautious of public appearances than Prince William - she reportedly had to remind him of how to conduct himself when out with friends, and had reportedly even taken it upon herself to ensure their privacy when going out. No matter how poised she was in public though, there was still no escaping the fact that Prince William had been right about placing his women in awkward positions – after all, what could a princess-in-waiting do, at the strange place between being a 'commoner' and the future King's wife?

Like Princess Diana before her, Kate was hounded by the press and sometimes ridiculed by the public, not excluding some classists in high English circles. Were she and her sister Pippa social climbers desperate to marry up? Was she lazy, or a gold-digger? How long does 'Waity Katie' really have to wait?

Much longer, as it turned out, for 2007 would give the couple and those rooting for them a scare. The couple was spending less time together, either because of William's commitments to his training, or by his preference to spend time with family and friends. There would be nights clubbing in London, with stories and sometimes photos to match that would prove hurtful and embarrassing to his girlfriend. By April 2007, the couple called it quits.

But Kate Middleton was a tough cookie and a smart woman. She gave William space and kept her quiet poise, but knew she would be photographed so she let her pictures speak a thousand words. She slipped on more chic clothing, went out more with her equally gorgeous sister Pippa, and showed the Prince just what he was missing. She also looked after herself well, and joined a group training for a charity dragon boat row. The sport gave her both ease of mind and a well-toned body. She was keeping busy and so was William, but behind the scenes, they were in contact and on the mend.

In just a few months the couple reunited, and for the next years went on as they always have – traveling, holidaying with each other's families and attending public events together. Amongst these key appearances were at William's graduation from the R.A.F in April 2008, and at the Garter ceremony later that year in June. Over the years, they found whatever time they could within the demands of their respective careers to be together; he was pursuing his military aspirations while Kate worked as an accessories buyer for the fashion brand, Jigsaw. She also did some work for the Middletons' party supplies business. But this wouldn't last for very long, as the couple would be engaged by October 2010.

William proposed while on a romantic holiday in Kenya, with a familiar blue stunner of a ring. The oval sapphire was surrounded by 14 solitaire diamonds, clocking in at 12-carats. The Garrard piece was previously owned by the groom-to-be's iconic mother, Princess Diana. After almost a decade of friendship and a pressure-cooker situation of a relationship, 'Waity Katie' was waiting no more, and Prince Charming was going to be her husband.

On April 29, 2011, the couple wed in a lavish ceremony watched by billions all over the world. On the occasion of his wedding, the Queen conferred on her grandson the title William, Duke of Cambridge. Kate

Middleton would thereafter be the Duchess of Cambridge – a fantastic departure from 'Waity Katie' indeed!

But William's life was that of unceasing pressure, and soon, attention would turn away from finding a bride, to making an heir. The perfect royal couple wouldn't disappoint on this score for very long, though. By late 2012, the official announcement of their first pregnancy is made, and George Alexander Louis – formally known as His Royal Highness Prince George of Cambridge - would be born months later in July 2013. He would be joined by a sister, Princess Charlotte Elizabeth Diana in May 2015, as well as a baby brother by April 2018.

By many accounts, William is a good father and a very hands-on one. He speaks openly of his love for their children and can be affectionate to them even in public. He is often seen carrying them in his arms or holding hands with them, and has confessed to fatherhood making him more emotional than he used to be. He is said to be determined to give his family stability and protection – and had even succeeded in petitioning for a no-fly zone over their home, Amner Hall, in Norfolk.

Not quite the concerns of a normal parent, but like any other mom and dad, Prince William had more conventional struggles too. A single father who snagged a chat with the Duchess of Cambridge at a charity event later revealed that Kate told him Prince William struggled early on too. The world got a peek of something like this firsthand in 2018, during a church service for Anzac Day. The event was held just a few days after Catherine gave birth to their third child, and William was caught on video struggling to stay awake. Many in the public took this to be symptomatic of life with a newborn baby and happily aired their support for the sleep-deprived dad of three!

A Life in Public Service

In unsubtle ways, being a royal was a literal job with financial contributions to the larger economy just by their very existence. They keep the wheels turning across industries and keep businesses running even by just the very content of their lives. They also promote their country outside of it, with effects on tourism and spending. William's role as bachelor prince, romantic Romeo and eventually, doting dad certainly fill the pages of papers and websites, feed TV ratings, spur tourism and sell merchandise. But existing alone is not enough. Royals can't just live their lives and expect to thus contribute. They need to be visible, they need to be accessible, and they are still expected to do some actual work, leveraging their public personas to push their advocacies and promote their charities, all while appearing to be politically neutral. There are sometimes very thin lines between these.

The extremely important visibility and work aspects of being a royal have been problematic when it comes to the otherwise uncontroversial Prince William. Indeed, other than the short-lived troubles he and Kate Middleton struggled with before getting engaged, he was sometimes considered boring, press-averse and work-shy. With a life settled with his Duchess and beloved family, then, what can we make of the Prince's other pursuits as a working royal?

Prince William had started university with an interest in the history of art, before finishing with geography. He then headed for military training, just like his brother Prince Harry. These are very diverse interests with differing paths, on top of his duties as a royal. So how does a talented man with plenty of prospects and privileges juggle all of these toward a career?

His time with the military showed him taking part in some very interesting operations. On the HMS *Iron Duke*, he participated in a multi-million-pound drug bust, seizing cocaine in the Caribbean Sea. He enjoyed flying too, and for a time was with the R.A.F. as a search-and-rescue pilot. At the time, in 2008, some in the press speculated his focus on his military career were just attempts to delay his official royal duties rather than serious pursuits. They certainly contributed to delays in his marriage to Kate, too.

Whether or not this was true cannot be proven. What seems clear though, is that William's romantic style and career focus shows a man who is headstrong and perhaps in his own way, also wise. Marriage and taking on official royal duties would have made any semblance of a "normal" life pretty much out of reach forever afterwards, why not give it more of a try? Besides, he has also seen how marrying so young could have been detrimental to his mom, so why not sow some wild oats, as the saying goes? As for career, what real rush was there to end his personal pursuits and trade them in for official duties? He was still behind his father, Prince Charles, in line to the throne – and

Charles himself had in some ways been adrift, spending most of his life trying to be useful while he waited for his own ascension. Why not nourish a career if he would just be standing in line behind the long-lived Windsors?

Taking Flight

Prince William would serve almost eight years in the military. When he was a Royal Air Force pilot involved in Search and Rescue, he was known to comrades as "Flight Lt. Wales." His position did not allow him to be involved in the riskiest of roles (his brother Harry, for example, would be allowed to do tours in Afghanistan), but he was well-liked, conducted himself professionally, and as a pilot, had direct contributions to saving lives, often in rough conditions. He left the military in 2013 shortly after the birth of his first son, George, but took on employment in the private sector in 2014 as a pilot for an air ambulance company (his salary was reportedly donated to charity).

For a while, he juggled fatherhood with work on top of his royal duties, until he ended his stint as a helicopter pilot for air ambulance services in 2017, so that he may finally devote himself fully to his royal duties and advocacies.

Work-Shy William?

William's seeming lack of commitment to his royal duties has been an issue for some time.

It must be remembered that his grandparents, Queen Elizabeth and her royal consort Prince Philip, have the constitution to continue working heavily even into their 90s. Over his royal life, for example, Prince Philip would go on to attend tens of thousands of engagements by the time he retired – at age 96!

A critical press isn't afraid to let the young Prince have it and some of them were bold enough to keep count and show receipts. One paper alleged the royal's first official engagement of 2016 was 47 days deep into the year, and even then it was a damaging one. At the height of the Brexit issue, a speech made by the Prince before the Foreign Office was construed as Pro-EU, which would have been a break from the royal's neutrality when it came to politics

(Kensington Palace thereafter denied it was a Pro-EU stand).

But it wasn't just the ruckus caused by the wording of his speech that was problematic to some royal watchers. At the time, his grandfather, over 94 years old at the time, was doing over 100 more engagements than he was. In one year, his public job count at home was 87 and 35 abroad, while in comparison, his grandfather was coming it at 250 and the Queen got up to as high as 341. In early 2017, he even missed Commonwealth Day services to go skiing and partying with friends. He had a job at the time as a pilot of course, and was a relatively new dad besides. But rumors were also swirling that he was a reluctant royal with more interest in being a gentleman farmer in the country or hanging out with his friends than carrying out his duties.

Prince William, who is a conservationist active in anti-poaching organizations, would also draw flak for advocating wildlife preservation while being an avid hunter (albeit of non-endangered and non-protected species).

In short, not only has he been doing little compared to others in his royal family, what he was doing was also not accomplished very well.

Certain members of the press had another axe to grind, too. Was the Prince being overly restrictive with media coverage of his family? Was he overstepping bounds in his attempts to control their coverage? The no-fly zone over their home earlier mentioned is just one manifestation of William's protective streak. They've limited press presence in certain events, not even bothering to distinguish tabloids from more reputable outlets. His staff is also known to be relentless with their complaints to and of the press, and the Prince has never been shy about his wariness of the media.

The Prince had always been open with his discomfort and distrust, but then again, why wouldn't he feel that way? To say that he has an understandable reserve would be an understatement. He saw his mother brought to tears by the press' constant attention, and their relentless pursuit had ultimately somehow contributed to her tragic death. He saw how getting a scoop could cause profound embarrassment and ridicule to his parents, and there was little he could do when the media gave his own future wife trouble while they were dating and she had no official designation or protection. His friends have been targeted too, and sometimes elaborately; there are reports of one of them being lured with a ruse on a business meeting that ended up with one of the attendees wired, and asking questions about William. Aggressive tactics directed at his children have been known too, with some behaviors bordering on stalking. Of course Prince William is going to be cautious.

The World Will Keep Watching

In a candid interview about accusations that he was work-shy, Prince William responded by saying he looked at his grandmother the

Queen as a role model for duty, and that he would eagerly take on tasks when they are given to him. He also seemed to have a good attitude about criticisms sent his way, saying he couldn't completely ignore them, nor does he take them "completely to heart."

For a man who can expect eyes to always be turned his way, and consequently an inability to please everyone – this actually seems to be a healthy way of looking at the world. He is a bright man and a circumspect one, who appears to give thought to his decisions and the ability to stick to them.

He saw by his mother's example that marrying young was hard; he sowed his wild oats and did things on his own time. He saw that royal roles could be restrictive, so he sought out ways to experience a "normal" life and pursue a career before committing himself to official duties. He had a rocky childhood, so he is doing his best to provide stability and protection for his own family.

Prince William has shown an ability to learn hard lessons and make careful moves from them. In some ways, he is "new" to a purely royal role. In some ways, he is "new" to his role as head of his own family. He might make early mistakes and bad moves. He may look work-shy and press-averse. But eventually, he is likely to find his stride. He is likely to find a way to balance understandable concerns for his family's safety and privacy, but also their need to be in the public eye in order to be effective at their job as royals. His history shows he can learn and find ways to grow and compromise, and settle into his roles be it as a student, a son, a husband, a father or, eventually, a King.

In the meantime, he *is* working.

He is a staunch protector of his mother's memory and legacy. In 2007, ten years after her death, William worked with his brother Prince Harry in a concert to raise funds for Princess Diana's charities. They've also participated in documentaries about her, often sharing very heartfelt and intimate details about what their mother was like in private, and their struggles with grief. The Prince is patron to many charities, and had always credited his family as heavy influencers in his sense of duty and responsibility. Amongst his causes are Centrepoint, which is focused on homeless youth; and the Tusk Trust, which works for wildlife preservation in Africa. Along with his brother, he established The Royal Foundation of the Duke and Duchess of Cambridge and Prince Harry, a vehicle for launching a variety of projects or increasing the impact and reach of existing projects and organizations that fit into their criteria, including the famous Invictus Games for wounded, ill and injured servicemen all over the world; the Heads Together Campaign, which advocates better approaches to mental health and fundraising for mental health initiatives; and a Cyberbullying taskforce. This is just a small slice of the kind of charity work that Prince William does. He is involved to varying degrees in many other causes, including wildlife conservation, AIDS & HIV, Cancer, Education, and Grief Support. Like his father, Prince William has also taken to writing to government ministers, though not so much on behalf of a cause or to lobby a position (which would have been against the royal family's usual neutrality) but to connect charities to people in government.

Yes, Prince William is working.

And as always, the world is watching closely.

Kate Middleton

The Commoner Who Would Be Queen

Michael Woodford

Introduction

In the lead up to the 20th anniversary of his mother's death, Prince Harry – brother in law to Kate Middleton – made some interesting observations about the monarchy.

He firstly said that the younger generation of royals feels that it is their role to modernize the monarchy.

In so doing, these royals believe, they will maintain its popularity and sustain its role for doing good.

They consider that, by bringing the House of Windsor into line with 21st century thinking, attitudes and lifestyles, they will enhance their own standing.

But not for selfish purposes, or for self-aggrandizement. No, for far more altruistic reasons.

They feel that from a position of trust and popularity they can do more to support charities, help the poor and suffering and improve the world.

These are noble aims, and are to be applauded.

But Harry said another thing in the interview.

In extending the idea of duty and responsibility to Great Britain, to the Commonwealth and, where possible, the world he recognized that one day one of the young royals would be monarch themselves.

It was just that, none of them wanted to do it.

They knew that they would have to, but just as hoovering the sitting room or putting out the bins has to be done but is not much fun, it is a necessary but unappealing job.

We can wonder whether this thought was anywhere in the mind of Kate Middleton, Berkshire lass, when she agreed to marry Prince William? And one day become his queen.

We might also consider how much she thought about the fact that everything she chose to do would be scrutinized, analysed and, often, criticized.

An Education

Tradition and heritage are important concepts to the Royal Family. After all, the line can be traced back far into history.

It was therefore understandable that Prince William should choose the third oldest educational institution in the English speaking world for his alma mater.

The University of St Andrews sits on the coast in the picturesque region of Fife, Scotland. The oldest of the four main universities in the country, it was the place where Kate and William met.

Rather in fitting with his mother's wish for her boys to see real life, St Andrews (as it is known) has one of the most diverse student bodies in the United Kingdom.

It is also a highly regarded institution, ranking only behind Oxford and Cambridge in terms of academic prowess.

Founded in 1410, it is home to a fraction over 10000 students. The town itself is only a little bigger in terms of population.

It was the seat of learning to a number of well-known personalities including, in recent times, politicians Alex Salmond and Michael Fallon.

Olympic champion cyclist Christ Hoy also attended the university. As did, joining in 2001, a certain couple who would soon dominate the pages of newspapers and magazines.

As well as the rapidly expanding fields of on line news and gossip.

They were not alone in discovering romance at the University – 1 in 10 students find their life partner there, a case of love and learning combining.

The old town stands just 60 miles to the north of Edinburgh in the quietest corner of Fife. So maybe there is little else to do but fall in love?

Certainly, the stunning landscapes, with sandy beaches and magnificent sea views, are the stuff of romantic novels.

The excellent restaurants, few, but of high quality, lend themselves to candlelit dinners and quiet chat over a glass of fine wine.

Perhaps they provide the answer to the University's success in matchmaking?

Or, of course, the famous St Andrew's golf links, home to events including the Open Championship.

The 'old course' is one of eleven in the immediate area. Its traditional old hotel would become a favorite haunt of the dating couple.

Before her death, Princess Diana (along with Prince Charles), had secured a degree of privacy from the media for their sons.

This would run through their education, giving them a small chance of enjoying some of the joys and challenges of school and university away from prying eyes.

Certainly, the boys had to cope with constant security, but, in return for the occasional managed story and photo session, they could get on with the early parts of their lives in relative quiet.

Something neither Charles nor, especially, Diana had enjoyed once they had met.

Kate and William, independently of the other, each opted to spend their first year at the University in the halls of residence.

Here they could get to know their peers, and establish friendships which would, as many do for university students, endure.

Sallies (St Salvator's Hall) looks like the stuff of dreams. Honeyed brick work and ivy clad walls, the coast just a short walk away. It is a destination in itself.

The phrase 'accommodation block' would be like calling Balmoral the country cottage.

Kate and William would undoubtedly have bumped into each other during their first year even had they had little in common. In fact, they shared many interests.

Sallies accommodates only 276 students, which includes its more modern annex, Gannochy House.

If the exterior of Sallies is wonderful, internally it is even more magnificent.

Although constructed relatively recently, (the 1930s), the enormous, oak beamed dining hall and stained-glass windows suggest more the baronial home of a Shakespearean Thane than student digs.

In fitting with a residence chosen by a royal, Sallies runs things in a very traditional way.

High Table operates once a week, when students are invited to join lecturers and other dignitaries for dinner. One suspects that this honor may have been extended to the future king.

Overlooking the edifice that is St Andrew's Castle, Sallies is a warmly welcoming place for its young inhabitants.

And if that description sounds like it has come from an upmarket holiday brochure, then fair enough. St Andrews and Sallies really are special places.

Kate's room was a couple of floors above William's, and the two often used to meet at the same time for breakfast. They soon discovered shared interests and traits.

Both were shy – William even considered pulling out of University - and by Christmas had become good friends. They shared a love of sport, and regularly went jogging and swimming together.

As often as Kate and William might have chatted on a jog, dined on the same table, or moaned about a particular assignment, it was in 2002 that the first seeds of a stronger relationship were sown.

A charity fashion event was taking place in the famous five-star hotel, Fairmont St Andrews, which was close to the university.

Kate was modelling at the event, and strode down the catwalk wearing a knitted dress.

The see-through garment was later sold for £78000.

Prince William was captivated. However, the meeting may never have happened.

Prior to gaining a place at St Andrews, Kate had in fact applied to another Scottish University, Edinburgh.

Quite late in the day, she changed her mind, although there was no certainty that she would get a place at the highly popular St Andrews.

Some think that it was a chance event that led her to actually seek to follow the future King to his university.   But this is unlikely.

However, some pupils from Marlborough (Kate's school) and Eton (William's place of learning) happened to meet up while both were still at school.

Parties involving the affluent children at boarding schools often take place in holiday times.

The friends are frequently spread around the country, so guests can come from far and wide.

Although both were at this particular gathering, along with the younger Prince Harry, there is no certainty that the two even spoke to each other.

Back in Scotland, following the seminal charity fashion show, the two (not yet a couple) decided to flat share for their second year at University.

Along with friends Fergus Boyd and Olivia Bleasdale, they rented a flat in a fine terrace in the town.

Although somewhat smaller than the homes they had grown up in, the building oozes traditional Scottish charm, with its long sash windows, ornate chimney stack and solid brick build.

Boyd, who drew William's attention to Kate at the charity show by whispering 'Wow, Kate's hot!' is an old Etonian friend of the Prince and was later made Godfather to Prince George.

Olivia Bleasdale also remained close friends with the couple, and was invited to their wedding.

However, the four were lucky to get the flat at all. Charlotte Smith, the landlady, had imposed a 'girls only' policy on letting the property.

She had rented it to a group of boys some years before, and they had left it in a state. Her worry was that, off the leash from their boarding school upbringing and year in halls, William and Fergus might let rip.

The girls had discovered the home, and when they raised the idea of sharing it with two boys, in a purely platonic sense, Smith had initially said no.

It was then revealed that one of the men was Prince William. Even at that point, Smith was unsure and decided to discuss it with her husband.

But, if you can't trust a prince, who can you trust? They talked it through with neighbors. After all, a member of the royal family comes with more baggage than just his cases.

But the neighbors were happy, and they agreed to let the flat. Apparently, the four students were ideal tenants, and did not even complain about the rent.

Mind you, we can reasonably assume it was well within their means to pay.

Kate was described by her landlady as very caring. Indeed, the whole group came across as a very nice collection of young adults.

It was during their time in the flat that Kate and William's friendship grew even closer, just beginning to edge into the romance that would lead to marriage.

If St Andrews as a town did not offer a huge range of entertainment, what it had was of good quality.

A favorite haunt was the Jahingir Indian restaurant. It was quite new back then, and a picture of its royal customer hangs in the curry house.

Today, a student special costs £9.95 and a Balti is available for under £12. Slightly different from the banquets the couple now attends.

Although the only electricity between the two still seemed to be the latent static from the thunderstorms rolling in off the North Sea, they did attend each other's 21st birthday bashes.

But then, one would expect no different of flatmates.

It was during their second year in the flat, and the third at St Andrews, that the friendship blossomed further. Christmas 2003 was the point that friends believed mutual love had burst through.

Their relationship was officially confirmed three months later, on April 1st 2004. Pictures of them skiing together at Klosters leaked out from paparrazi spies and the relationship had to be announced.

The couple then moved out of the flat for their final year, sharing a cottage on the edge of the town.

With their finals approaching (both would eventually graduate with 2:1s) work began to take precedence over romance but the two were again seen at Klosters, and at the 56th birthday for William's father.

The event at Highgrove for Charles was a relatively private affair.

After university, William demonstrated his mother's attitude of wanting more from life than just that of a working royal by deciding to follow a career in the military.

Whilst it was always traditional for male royals to follow this route, in his case, it was a genuine career choice.

However, things were tougher for Kate. She was and was not a part of the royal set up.

Whilst she had the down side of the press interest in everything she did, she did not yet get the level of protection and screening that her boyfriend enjoyed.

A bit part job in the clothing chain, Jigsaw (which was owned by a family friend) was followed by returning to work in her parents' business, Party Pieces. In the meantime, she waited. And waited.

William's career was taking off – literally, he would become a flying officer – but Kate was caught between her own life and the pressures of being associated with the second in line to the throne.

When William enrolled into Sandhurst, the officers' training ground, they knew that opportunities for time together would be limited during the year long course.

Following his training, William was commissioned and became an officer in the Blues and Royals (following his younger brother, who did not attend university).

Pressure was mounting on the couple, and at an event at Cheltenham racecourse, they seemed cold towards each other.

Revelations then followed that William had been seen dancing with another woman at a nightclub.

The couple had shared a cooling off period during their final year at university, but had got back together quickly.

This time, with the two more mature, the problems seemed deeper. Kate, though, took the opportunity to enjoy herself.

Dressing up, partying and generally having a good time. Going out with her sister,

Pippa. She began to find much needed breathing space.

And, as the saying goes, absence made the heart grow fonder. Three months later, the two were once more a couple.

Even better for getting away from the incessant attention, they set up home on island of Anglesey, where William's work as a search and rescue pilot took them.

The pair rented a four-bedroomed whitewashed cottage in the Welsh speaking hamlet of Bordorgan, which is in the south west of the tiny island.

The owner, George Meyrick, was well known to royals, and used to invite the couple into his own home, a stately pile, for shepherd's pie and claret.

Having been spoiled by the scenery in Scotland, they found the views from Anglesey just as spectacular. Their farmhouse overlooked a small beach and was wonderfully isolated.

Although the location was meant to be kept secret, for security reasons, it was widely known on the island and because a tourist attraction for visitors, albeit an unofficial one.

The couple settled comfortably and, almost certainly, with relief into the quiet community.

And there was clearly something in the fresh Welsh air, because just four months after they arrived, William proposed and Kate accepted.

They holidayed in Kenya (where William actually popped the question) but back in Wales, although their home was isolated, they were on friendly terms with locals when they saw them.

They would often stop for a chat. Kate liked to shop in Homebased, buying cute items for their home (no antique furnishings with historical associations then).

William would leave for work - his security team in close attendance – regularly at a quarter to seven. Occasionally, his work helicopter would collect him.

Kate would shop, buying fish for dinner and trawling the local Waitrose, protection officer trying to blend seamlessly into the background.

There were no heirs and graces, the couple dressing casually and committing to their new home environment.

Visits to the cinema and surfing would occupy their leisure time. Occasionally, the young couple would return to the follies of their student days.

On one occasion they dressed up in silly wigs and costumes in order to get incognito into the cinema. Unfortunately, in staid Anglesey, they stood out even more than normal.

Another attempt at disguise saw them riding around in a white van, and motor biking through the scenic country lanes was another past time.

When they finally left Anglesey – by this time married – it was with great sadness. Sadness to themselves and the locals.

By this time William's posting was over, but the residents say that they are always welcome to return.

As for the cottage, that was not put back onto the market. But, rather like the flat in

Hope Terrace, St Andrews, it was left in immaculate order.

Even the gym equipment that filled one of the bedrooms left no marks. It was an astonishingly ordinary spell of time for the future wife of the King of England and wonderful for that.

If locals were treated kindly, others had a harder time.

A sky TV repairman had arrived on the island to sort something for the Rupert Murdoch owned company.

But, and we have all been here, his Sat Nav took him to the wrong place. Driving down a winding track, he was suddenly pounced up by black suited protection officers.

He must have thought he had been transported to one of the American action movies his employer so often broadcast.

'You look incredible Beautiful'

April 29th, 2011 - The date of the wedding of Kate Middleton to Prince William.

Thirty years previously, when his parents had married, the superlative claims had seemed justified.

'Marriage made in heaven' and 'fairy tale marriage' were not just hyperbole, but the genuine belief of a nation who saw royalty as different and rather special.

We know more these days, and as splendid as the occasion was, there was no intention of setting the couple up for a fall.

But with the economy in freefall thanks largely to the Arab spring, and Syria entering civil war, the world needed something to lift their spirits.

And when it comes to pomp, splendor and tradition, nobody quite does it like the British.

Two billion people tuned in for the wedding, a brief glimpse of the sun in a cloudy world.

Kate had kept the details of her dress secret. Designed by Sarah Burton as a part of the Alexander McQueen fashion dynasty, the ivory and lace dress set off her looks to perfection.

As well, it enthralled the fashion industry, causing more fizz than an over shaken bottle of bubbly.

Her ring, which was a tight fit and a struggle to put on - the only moment of anxiety during the ceremony - was of classic Welsh gold, and had been given to the Prince by his grandmother.

It was very much a British occasion.

Nineteen hundred guests crowded into Westminster Abbey, with hundreds of thousands outside. It went without a hitch.

From the 1902 royal landau which took the couple from the ceremony, to the lunchtime reception hosted by the Queen, the event had to be perfect, and it was.

Kate wore a diamond encrusted tiara, lent by the Queen, which gave her the appearance of a Princess.

But by making her grandson Duke of Cambridge, the Queen had made Kate a duchess. Perhaps there were too many bad historical memories left in the term 'Princess'.

During the ceremony itself, a prayer – written by the now Royal couple – was read out. Otherwise, the service was un-notable.

Afterwards, the journey amongst the throngs passed through Parliament Square, beyond

Whitehall and onto Horse Guards Parade. It was cheered at every trot.

Down the Mall and into the Palace went the couple, waving and smiling, and onto the Reception hosted by the Queen.

Crowds had been queuing for hours – days in some cases – to get the best views and they were rewarded at 1.30, when they saw what they had come for.

Kate and William appeared on the Buckingham Palace balcony and kissed before the cheering masses.

A fly past followed, with a World War Two Lancaster bomber guarded by two spitfires rumbling over the Palace to cheers and roars.

Tornado and Typhoon jets followed. The newly appointed Duke, pointing out the planes to his smiling wife, offered a second kiss.

A clear sense prevailed that this was a chance to celebrate and show off the nation, its present and its past.

As much as she must have been expecting the enormous reaction, Kate (now Duchess of Cambridge) was seen to murmur 'Oh my' as she saw the cheering public.

The day finished more privately, with the Prince of Wales hosting a private dinner for close friends and family.

It had been a mixture of the pomp and privacy that the royals manage with great skill.

Motherhood

The newer generations of royals are fulfilling their aim and their duty as they see it, to address the challenges and problems facing us all.

Included amongst these for young parents, mothers especially, are mental health issues.

Kate admits that, even with the levels of support to which she has access, being a mother is really difficult.

As she says, despite all the advice you can get (wanted, or otherwise) a lot of the time you just make it up as you go along.

This is especially true as she coped with two pre-school aged children. This sense of not being sure that your decisions are right, or if you should be handling matters differently, can really impact on a mum.

It can lead to feelings of loneliness and inadequacy, leading on to full scale depression.

By talking about such mental health concerns, and showing that a duchess is as susceptible to them as anybody, Kate hopes to demystify these previously hidden illnesses.

By bring them into the open; she hopes that people will feel more confident talking about their feelings, their worries. Thus, they will be more willing to get help.

Of course, her children's grandmother, Diana, suffered enormously from depression through William's early years, only revealing publicly her problems shortly before her death.

Kate and William have two children. George was born on 22nd July 2013, with his sister Charlotte joining the world on May 2nd 2015.

Her pregnancy with George was not an easy one, and resulted in an earlier than usual public announcement.

She had been admitted to hospital and, of course, the press had a field day spreading rumor and promoting assumption.

The couple felt it better to announce the pregnancy, and reveal that the hospital attendance was to cope with extreme morning sickness, than to let the rumors continue apace.

It would be nice to say that the Duchess's second pregnancy was easier, but the unborn Charlotte caused as much nausea as her brother.

Had they been born the other way round, with Charlotte appearing first, then the birth would have made history.

Following centuries of male primogeniture (male children surpassing their older sisters in the order of heirdom to the throne), the Government had decided to move the royals forward a century or ten.

It is now the first born who becomes heir, irrespective of whether this is a boy or a girl.

George will soon be starting his formal education; his parents have chosen one of the independent St Thomas's schools in London.

This fits very much with William's own upbringing. Diana, with Charles agreeing, forewent the tradition of using private tutors for their children's early years.

This was in line with the young princes gaining as normal a childhood as possible, using the tube and visiting London Zoo.

Given that William and Kate are seeking to modernize the monarchy, it seems likely that their children will follow a route that many other children of wealthy parents take.

So what are the possible educational paths of George, Charlotte and any other children the couple might have?

Despite the wish to give their children as normal an upbringing as possible, it seems highly unlikely that they would completely break with tradition and use state schools.

That might just be a step too far.

The Thomas's group of schools, to which George is enrolled, takes children up to the age of 13 in two of their branches.

Thomas' are day schools, and commutable from the couple's Kensington Palace home. However, even William and his brother Harry attended boarding schools from a young age.

Whether the children will do the same will be one of the first key decisions the parents have to make.

If the children follow in the footsteps of recent generations and develop a passion for sport and the outdoors, then a move out of London might be on the cards.

That would mean one of three things: the whole family moves, but this could cause problems with the growing state duties that Kate and William incur.

Secondly, the young children could commute. Increasing numbers of youngsters do this. There is a huge growth in the number of Prep Schools just outside the M25 who offer a mixture of boarding and day facilities.

Possibly 'flexi-boarding' could be the answer, giving the children more time at home but also an introduction to boarding. This would, to a degree, satisfy tradition.

Finally, of course, the children could follow the traditional route of joining a full boarding prep school.

The last option opens up William's old place of learning, Ludgrove (in Wokingham) as a possibility. The school certainly is secluded, which makes security easier to handle.

But only for George, as it is an all-boys school.

Cheam, where Prince Charles and George's great uncles went, is another possibility. With a strong reputation for care, and a location just outside Newbury, it is close enough for him to get home for weekends off.

Mind you, these 'exeat' breaks are only occasional through the term, lessons and sport usually taking place on a Saturday.

There is a further question for our modernizing royals to consider. Should their children attend single sex or co-educational schools?

There are plenty of both from which to choose. Perhaps an option such as St George's Windsor might fit the bill.

The school has a royal heritage – Princess Beatrice is a past pupil – and its attachment to Windsor Castle means that Great Granny and Grandad might look after the kids.

The same question remains for the senior school, which usually begins at 13 for those educated privately.

Day Schools in London, such as St Paul's and City of London offer single sex day education.

Or maybe they will follow in their parents' footsteps. Eton for George and Marlborough for Charlotte.

Whatever the choices might be, we can be fairly sure that the young royals have their names on a waiting list already. And they are unlikely to be turned down.

Another consideration is that the very traditional schools that Princes Charles, and older generations, attended either no longer exist, or have changed out of all recognition.

He described Gordonstoun as 'Colditz in Kilts'; the school is far more welcoming today. Eton is no longer just a bastion of wealth and privilege (although plenty of that remains).

Rather, it is a multi-cultural school which, through its extensive bursaries, takes boys from a variety of backgrounds. It is often at the forefront of educational ideas.

Whereas at Prince Charles' Prep School, Hill House, marching formed a part of the curriculum until recently. (Apparently, something to do with insufficient rooms for the pupils.)

Times have changed.

So, whatever option has been chosen, Kate and William's children will get a taste of something akin to normal life.

At least, normal for one born into wealth and opportunity.

In another break from tradition, but one which echoes William's upbringing under Princess Diana's influence, the young children have already participated in an overseas tour.

George was just three and his sister still toddling when they accompanied their parents on an official visit to Canada.

Of course, the reaction from the Canadian public at seeing the youngsters was ecstatic.

Diana had taken William to Australia on tour when he was a baby, but only after a huge battle with the palace, who felt he should be looked after by nannies.

The children have also been page boy and bridesmaid at their Aunt's wedding. The youngsters stole the show at Pippa Middleton's event.

Mind you, George had a bit of a tantrum during the long drawn out service, getting himself told off by his mum. It's reassuring that even royal children have their moments.

Perhaps he was following in his father's footsteps? William was only a little older when he went to his Uncle Andrew's wedding.

At that event he pulled faces, looked extremely cross and was reluctant to hold hands with his fellow assistant. To be fair, though, that was a girl! (His cousin, Laura Fellowes).

Growing Up

Kate, or Catherine as she is actually named, is not a typical bride for a future king. Although from a very comfortable middle-class family, she is not connected to the royalty.

That makes her an unusual, but not unheard of, choice.

Her father's family had distant ties to the aristocracy, which gave access to some trust funds. These helped financially when she was younger.

Her parents originally worked in the aviation industry. Her father was a flight despatcher and her mother a flight attendant.

Later, they set up a highly successful business, which is now worth tens of millions of pounds.

Catherine (her name was shortened to Kate only when she moved to University) was christened in Bradfield, Berkshire after her Reading birth.

This was on January 9th 1982. It is highly unlikely that her midwife would have suspected how famous the new born would become.

Bradfield is a delightful little village, dominated by the boarding college of the same name. Indeed, this whole area of England, full of rolling hills, green fields and south of the Thames is delightful.

And rather well off.

Working for British Airways, the family was posted to Jordan, in the Middle East, when Kate was just two.

The family spent two years there, and Kate attended an English speaking nursery.

On their return to England, the family moved to Chapel Row, a tiny hamlet near Bucklebury, which lies just to the south of the M4 and east of Newbury.

From there, she joined St Andrews Prep School in Pangbourne.

The school shares some characteristics with her future husband's Prep, Ludgrove. Both are set rurally, near small towns.

Each caters for the children of the wealthy, and is traditional in its outlook.

Both are accessed down a long drive, making them seem more remote from the real world than they actually are.

St Andrews is, though, co-educational and, unlike the all-boys Ludgrove, has optional rather than compulsory boarding.

Kate's family took advantage of this, and she was mostly a day pupil who boarded with increasing regularity when she was older.

Separated by under twenty miles it is more than likely that the future couple would have inadvertently met, if not spoken, at some school event of other.

Perhaps a time when Ludgrove boys visited the school for a fixture, maybe for a musical event or theatre experience.

Kate was, like the family she would join, interested in sports. She was a fine athlete, and held the school high jump record for a number of years.

She left St Andrews when 13, and moved to Downe House near Newbury. Unfortunately, the change of school did not work out for her.

The girls' only atmosphere allied with the fact that she was a naturally shy person meant that she found it hard to fit in.

Quite quickly, she became a target for bullying. Indeed, the impact of the two terms that she spent at Downe House in the mid-1990s may have come out later.

At her wedding, she requested that the guests make contributions to, amongst others, an anti-bullying charity. This in place of the superfluous need for normal gifts.

The then Head teacher, Susan Cameron, preferred the term 'teasing' to bullying. But whatever, the culprits and indeed the facts of the events have remained secret.

Sporty pupils like Kate often get on well with their peers, but equally girls in their early teens can be thoughtless in their comments.

Miss Cameron told a British newspaper that she thought Kate was unhappy and unsettled, but not the recipient of serious bullying.

But, victims would say that bullying is bullying. The action of singling out one child or a group of children, for continued nastiness is deeply upsetting to the victims.

That Kate remained at her Prep School until the end, whereas girl only schools often transfer their pupils at 11, meant that friendship groups were already established.

This may also have made the settling in period more challenging than normal.

In addition, Kate was an especially strong hockey player, but had little experience of playing the school's main sport, lacrosse.

For somebody who had been top of her tree at prep school to suddenly move down the pecking order can be hard. Especially when there is unpleasantness – no, let us avoid euphemism - bullying around.

Downe House features a number of well-known alumni, including sports presenter Clare Balding, comedy actress Mirandha Hart and model Sophie Dahl.

But Kate used to cry herself to sleep there. However, Miss Cameron's take on the experience is interesting.

She believed that it helped turn Kate into the strong lady that she is today. Others might see longer term effects of bullying, or teasing if you prefer, as more negative.

In fact, as extremely harmful, the notion that it is character building is quite outdated.

However, Kate managed to secure a place at Marlborough School. Here, life was much better for her, and echoed more her time at St Andrews.

She was known still as being quiet, but was hard working, popular and extremely sporty. She was also quite down to earth, and became one of the crowd.

Past pupils include the singer Chris De Burgh, poets John Betjeman and Siegfried Sassoon and Sally Bercow, wife of the Speaker of the House of Commons.

The spy Anthony Blunt also attended Marlborough.

Rather like William's extremely old-fashioned attire at Eton, Marlborough includes oddities amongst its uniform, including a long black skirt.

However, in the full boarding community, there was, and remains, a mix of backgrounds.

Parties in stately homes, polo and other evidence of the privilege of wealth are common, but so are the children whose parents scraped together the fees (now over £30000 per annum) and lived a relatively austere life as a result.

Kate did well at the school and her results put her in a position to choose the university that appealed most to her.

She gained excellent grades in her A level subjects, which were Chemistry and Biology, along with Art.

However, before higher education, like many teenagers with the backing and independence to do so, she took a gap year.

In effect, this was two gap 'half years', combining time in Italy with a trip to Patagonia.

The gap year would be a chance to de-stress after her A levels and gain some life experiences that she could draw upon as she got older.

Given the direction her life would take, this might well have proved to be a good decision.

She began the year with an intensive twelve week course at the British Institute in the beautiful Italian city of Florence.

This would give her a chance to develop her love of art, learning about the great works in the city. Also, she would be able to explore the culture of this, one of the world's great destinations.

Following Florence, she decided to take on a physically and emotionally much tougher challenge. She would participate in an Operation Raleigh working visit to Chile.

Although she did not know it at the time, her decision was an omen towards the direction her life was soon to take.

Prince William had been on the same excursion just weeks before. He had loved the experience, and, had Kate simply swapped the order of her gap year experiences, they could well have met then.

Her group consisted of 150 young people from all walks of life, with many being wealthy young men and women who had also recently finished their A levels at boarding school.

But the party also included teenagers from more normal backgrounds as well as young offenders who were given the opportunity to use the experience to get their lives back on track.

Those who had recently been in drug rehabilitation programs were also on the trip.

Climatic conditions in Patagonia would be, at the time of year they travelled (British winter), similar to a British Autumn. Lingering warmth would be countered by a lot of rain.

Kate took work on the boat, BT Global Challenge, where her duties included everything from chatting with guests to cleaning and helping with deck duties such as lowering the ship's sails.

After that, she developed her knowledge with work in the field of science. She assisted on projects collecting organisms and analyzing sea life for conservation purposes.

She was seen, rather as in her school days, as a hardworking, strong and athletic person who got on with her duties willingly and without any fuss.

She seemed determined to get the absolute most out of her experience.

Another skill that Kate was beginning to exhibit was her ability to relate to children. She was successful in helping out in a local school, teaching English.

Kate had grown into a very beautiful young lady, who got on well with boys as well as girls. But, according to the leaders of the trip, she was never of the slightest trouble to them.

After they were married, Kate and William were able to thank the Operation Raleigh staff and volunteers in a small way. They met a group at a project in Borneo.

From her gap year, Kate moved on to University. Her original choice had been to study History of Art at Edinburgh, but, of course, she swapped, completing her education at St Andrews.

Various claims have been made that this was so that she could be at the same venue as

Prince William, whose choice was announced before she changed her mind.

However, many students alter their destination, and the appeals of both St Andrews and Edinburgh are considerable, if different.

Edinburgh University is set in the heart of the city, at the center of a large cultural and financial hotspot.

Whilst its view down the Royal Mile to the Firth of Forth is, on a sunny day, of great magnificence, the city is more renowned for its architecture.

Edinburgh is a great university, but its reputation for art is not as high as that of St

Andrews. And, it has over three times as many students as the Fife institution.

For a quiet girl, who had grown up in countryside settings and who had spent much of her gap year developing her love of her subject, to swap was not such an odd choice to make.

Miners, Kings and Party Pieces

Kate was five when her mum realized that she had a difficulty that could well be shared by many others in the country.

With two very young children, plus another on the way, and living in an affluent area, birthday parties were a bit of a problem. And, in particular, what to put in the bags at the end of the day.

Sweets and tat were the only real options beyond a slice of birthday cake.

Inspiration was provided for the Middleton family business, Party Pieces. From humble beginnings in the garden shed, the company took off big time.

As it expanded, Kate's father Michael gave up his job as a flight despatcher and joined in, then more and more employees. The business outgrew its shed and moved a nearby farm.

Selling balloons, bunting, cakes, confetti and almost anything else you can imagine connected with parties, the business certainly benefitted from Kate's royal connections.

Visits to its website increased by over 160% in the week the couple's wedding was announced, and having a link to the House of Windsor definitely helped with credibility.

Carole Middleton, Kate's mother, is undoubtedly a driven person. Whether as an entrepreneur or in supporting her children, she is a conspicuous figure.

She grew up in more humble surroundings than she now enjoys and attended her local state schools.

Tracing back far enough, and with enough convenient marriages and leaps of faith, her lineage can be tracked to Edward IV, who was King of England in the 15th Century.

But that her great grandfather was a Durham miner is a better indication that Carole is very much not of blue blooded heritage.

Now, however, her heritage is reflected on the golden chevron on the coat of arms given to the couple. Her maiden name is Goldsmith.

Her nature is such that from time to time press coverage of Carole Middleton has been less than flattering.

Stories that she has driven Kate into various decisions to manipulate her relationship with William and the royals abound.

She has been accused of encouraging Kate to disregard royal traditions by having a significant say in the procedures she follows.

Included amongst these are the arrangements around her bodyguard, and whether it should be a man or woman.

She was accused of being behind Kate's decision to change universities to be with William at St Andrews.

Currently, she is apparently encouraging Kate, whose two pregnancies so far have been difficult, to have another child.

There have been many other stories, linking alleged problems in the royal marriage back to Carole and making miles out of meters regarding royal treats, such as access to the royal box at Wimbledon.

Allegations of poor relations with the House of Windsor are manifold in the tabloids and on-line gossip sites. And so on.

But there are many counter points to be considered. Firstly, in the age in which we live, there is in no reason why a husband's family should have a greater input into a marriage than a wife's.

It wouldn't happen in a marriage where the husband is not a prince, so there is no reason why it should when he is one.

Secondly, most of the stories are without much basis, relying on rumor and unsubstantiated leaks. On top of this, we all know that the media loves a bit of gossip.

Thirdly, there is absolutely no reason why Kate, who has a strong relationship with her mother, should not call on her for advice and guidance.

After all, the record of the royals with regards to William's mother is unimpressive, although things have changed. Carole has made a more than decent job with her own three children.

The younger royals talk frequently about modernizing the monarchy, making it truer to real life. Letting a young mother seek advice from her own mum is an example of them doing this.

If Carole's link to any royal heritage is so tenuous as to have no real substance, then her husband's link to aristocracy is a little closer – although still pretty distant.

However, the connections did mean that he grew up comfortably, with trust funds providing income for the family.

He has a direct link to King Edward III, who ruled in the thirteen hundreds, but closer, his grandmother – Olive – was an aristocrat.

Unlike his wife, Michael did attend an independent school, Clifton College in Bristol.

Kate has two siblings, Pippa and James, the latter followed her to Marlborough whilst

Pippa went to Downe House, where her more outgoing personality meant that she had a much happier time than her sister.

Of the two, Pippa is more regularly in the news.

Classified as a 'socialite', she married in 2017. She is also a columnist and author. And has, like her sister, worked in the family business.

James is an entrepreneur who has created more than one company. He is active in raising awareness about his learning difficulty, dyslexia.

A Much-Maligned Duchess

An awful lot of people are happy to offer their views on Kate Middleton.

This probably results from mixture of her position and that (relatively speaking) she has come from a standing of ordinariness to royalty, inspiring just a dusting of jealousy.

Also, people's willingness to cast views and aspersions on who they wish is just how things are in latter part of the 2010s.

Social media means that many hold a view on everything, and (seemingly) it doesn't matter how we express it.

The result is a see saw of positive and negative reports and comments.

Perhaps it is the Diana effect, but the public feels that they have the right to know everything a royal does.

At the same time, not all views expressed about Kate are negative, far from it.

And she is influential. Just by becoming wife of a future king, she was described by Time Magazine as one of the planet's most significant people.

Perhaps being the first royal wife to hold a university degree is a part of that.

But this positive note is countered by the negativity displayed around her wearing 25 outfits on a week-long tour to Canada.

Is that really such an excessive amount for a nine-day visit?

She is clearly an icon for fashion, just like Diana before her; a dress she wore generated such interest that they sold at a rate of one a minute after she was photographed in it.

But signing a pre-nuptial agreement is seen as bad. She is presented as 'one of us' shopping in Waitrose and Tescos, buying ingredients for the cooking she loves to do.

But her parenting skills are scrutinized by the public and in the press.

This up and down relationship with the public is reflected in, or maybe led by, her relationship with the media.

Certainly, she can become frustrated with photo sessions and lengthy media occasions. But sometimes coverage of her has gone too far.

From the early days, post university, it has been a love hate relationship. A part of the problem might be that Kate and William are considered celebrities as much as royals.

And that means, in the eyes of many, that they are open to as much scrutiny as anybody chooses to give them.

With so many platforms on which to broadcast 'news', a never ending supply is needed.

If that dries up, it is seen as legitimate to speculate and hypothesise in a negative way. Hence the unevidenced guesswork into the royal couple's parenting skills.

There have been specific events which have undermined Kate's trust in the media. In 2012, a French magazine printed grainy photographs, taken from a huge distance, of her sunbathing topless on a beach.

Something completely normal for the setting in which it occurred.

Even more disturbing, given heightened security fears over terrorist actions around the world, two paparazzi recently followed Prince George when he was playing in the park with his nanny.

The sense is there that the royals cannot win – criticized if they put up the covers and are viewed as distant from the populace, but exploited when they do appear, informally, in public.

If Kate can become angry at the intrusion into private matters by the press, then her husband is even more determined to keep them a minimum.

He considers legal action appropriate for unwanted and unwarranted intrusion. Of course, he experienced the suffering his mother went through at the invasive nature of the media.

In addition, he will have in his thinking the skiing holiday in Klosters in 2005.

At this event, his father had forgotten that he was wired up, and broadcast his views about the BBC correspondent, Nicholas Witchell – an 'awful' man, according to Charles' comment.

And a Daily Mail journalist wormed her way into the young royals' party set, only to reveal all to the nation.

Perhaps unsurprisingly, the press is not welcome on their holidays.

Kate, too, has won damages for their unceasing intrusions.

However, the media see it differently. They feel that the royal couple needs to understand that the public are interested in them, and as such they should allow more access.

British papers become frustrated as they largely fall in line with the requests of the palace but see their overseas colleagues publishing freely abroad.

Certainly, viewing footage of the pressure put on Kate before her marriage is disturbing.

Hordes of paparazzi chase her down the street, sometimes on motorcycles, and flash photography explodes in her face. At times she is almost pushed to the ground such is the mindless desire for a close up.

It does not engender good relationships. Comments from senior journalists along the lines that the public 'need to know', and the only way to prove a story is to get the photo, seems self-serving.

It has created the situation where royals of William and Kate's generation are seeking to take control of their own media stories.

Kate used The Huffington Post, an online blogging news site, to promote her relationship with a mental health charity.

At the same time royal correspondents, flavor of the month so recently at the Queen's Jubilee celebrations, now fear for their jobs.

They suspect that social media will become the main platform for royal stories in the future. Of course, in a way, that is a return to the old days of the public just being told 'what is good for them'.

At the same time, many of the paparazzi can only blame themselves for the situation.

Trusted photographers are permitted at private events. But many of the photographs released of the royal children are taken by Kate herself, and distributed via social media.

Shock, horror. After all, it is unheard of for mums to proudly publish photographs of their children on social sites! Especially if they are, as is Kate, keen amateur photographers.

The press speaks cynically of 'Middleton Rules', the conditions created by William and Kate's father around what might or might not be published.

But then this might be a reasonable response to being called 'work-shy' and the 'invisible princess' by some British papers.

It seems as though the press want it both ways. They urge the royals to be more normal, more accessible, but then exploit the freedom this gains.

They seem to forget that in the pre-Diana days, whilst the royal correspondents might have been more accepted, the stories they were offered were stage managed.

And the press seems to have lost track of the fact that times have moved on.

Whilst they might need photos of a smiling Prince George to sell papers, the Cambridge family does not need the press to share their message.

The world is changing.

Although, of course, the press might not agree.

Royal Relationships

The Queen warmed quickly to her grandson's girlfriend and that relationship has stayed strong throughout the couple's subsequent marriage.

She is, naturally enough, particularly fond of the two great grandchildren, George and Charlotte, and leaves gifts for them when she visits.

However, despite the generally positive feelings the two shows for each other, there have been times when matters between Kate and her monarch have become strained.

The Queen is, of course, renowned for her work ethic and her belief in duty above all.

When Kate was struggling with her health during her pregnancies, bad feeling did bubble up.

Kate had a particularly severe form of morning sickness, and anybody who has experienced this knows how debilitating it can be.

It resulted in her missing a number of public events and whilst there was sympathy from the head of the household at the outset, the Queen did feel that enough was enough.

That Kate should get out of her sickbed and return to complete her engagements. William, though, was worried that a too early return to work could have longer term health implications.

There was also a small dispute over George's first birthday party. The Queen offered the formal setting of Balmoral but Kate chose instead to hold the event in their London apartment.

She felt that the youngster would have more fun at home.

Even though niggles such as this might from time to time arise, it is very little different from many homes where an elderly matriarch cannot quite come to terms with how the young ones behave.

Another area of concern between the two is also generational. The Queen from time to time expresses doubts over Kate's choice of dress.

Whilst many would disagree over the older royal's views, Kate is seen as a style icon. Her style receives endless coverage especially when stretching royal protocol.

On occasion, her clothes have been regarded as too revealing for the position she holds.

But despite these odd disagreements, Kate describes the Queen as a calming, gentle and wise influence in her life, and that of her children.

The relationship Kate has with her father in law and Camilla Parker Bowles is also generally strong with occasional moments of conflict.

Inevitably, frictions that do occur tend to be over the grand children, and have focused more on the role played by Kate's parents than the couple themselves.

However, Kate and William have worked hard to ensure that there are equal opportunities for all the grandparents to play their part.

It is, though, extremely difficult to avoid the pernickety criticisms seen in the press when every aspect of their lives is scrutinized.

One of the royals with whom Kate shares a laugh is Prince Phillip.

Although she and William do not always attend the usual royal celebrations at

Sandringham (don't most couples share around the Christmases?) the elderly Phillip is well known for his, admittedly un-PC, and sense of humor.

William holds a close tie with his brother Harry, and Kate too is fond of her younger brother in law.

The pair shares a sense of humor, and Harry is particularly good with his niece and nephew.

Living close to his brother and sister in law, they often meet, sharing a meal or a session watching Game of Thrones.

Kate also provides a sisterly influence in his life, and has been a great advisor over

Harry's romance with the actress Meghan Markle.

In particular, she has passed on her experiences of coping with the media attention.

When pictured together, usually with William making up the three, Harry and Kate exhibit a clear warmth and friendship. Kate looks more relaxed than when in more formal situations.

The three have also worked together on charities, most notably recently launching the Heads Together mental health organization with which the two brothers have strong personal ties.

Another royal with whom Kate gets on particularly well is the Countess of Wessex, Sophie.

The two share their 'commoner' backgrounds, and also a love of shopping. They are often seen at Wimbledon in each other's company.

Zara Tindall's love of sports draws her close with both Kate and William. She is George's Godmother, and at royal gatherings they will usually gravitate together.

Perhaps two of the royals with whom there is less of a natural bond are Princesses Beatrice and Eugenie.

However, there are no problems between the children of Prince Andrew and Kate, more that they share less in common.

The challenge of joining a family such as the Windsors is that they are more than just a family. They are an institution and one that is in the public eye.

Meeting the family is difficult for any outsider, and Kate seems to have made a decent fist of it. Inevitably, and very typically, there will have been some tensions.

But these are normal, it is just that for most they are not scrutinized and shared by outsiders.

Similarly, Kate's parents are often criticized as though, because they are commoners, they somehow have less to offer.

And less right to be involved. In fact, William, Harry and their generation have stressed their wish to continue the work their mother, inadvertently, began.

Now the princes are old enough to make a difference, they have gone about the modernization process which is essential for the good of the monarchy.

Kate has played her part, in often very difficult circumstances, in all of this.

Troubled Times

It is interesting to scan through some of the online gossip – nonsense might be a better word – that emerges around Kate and William's marriage.

One unnamed site uses two vastly different and unrelated quotes to form an article which more or less declares the marriage over.

On the one hand is unsubstantiated rumor that Kate was pregnant with her third child, but had not announced it (at the time of the article, she decidedly was not pregnant).

This is then linked to a comment overheard by a teenager who saw Prince William on a tour to New Zealand.

Asked how many children he would like, he smilingly says 'Two'. He is hardly likely to say another number, given the headlines that would cause.

The teenager reports this back to the media. Such is the basis for the fact that the couple are in marital trouble. Kate is pregnant with child number 3 (she isn't) and William doesn't want it (there's nothing to want).

With a rare sense of self scrutiny, this particular outlet realizes that the story is, to put it mildly, thin. So, to back up the point, reference is made to their up and down times during courtship.

And to seal the deal, it manages to twist that fact that the couple is seen together in public, apparently deeply fond of each other and having a good time, as further proof of a break up.

Clearly, the article claims, being seen jointly in public only occurs to dampen down rumors of a split. Apparently, the Queen has 'ordered' the two to appear together.

Against this type of over-hyped nonsense, it is impossible to draw accurate conclusions. It would be a strange marriage if there were not, from time to time, disagreements.

But let us try to look at the facts. It was widely reported that Kate moved out of London and back with her parents whilst she was pregnant with Charlotte.

This was assumed, in some quarters, to be evidence of a separation.

That depends on how you interpret the word. In the most literal sense, William and his wife were separate for a spell. Just as they are if he undertakes royal duties alone.

We know that Kate was extremely ill during her pregnancy. We know that their London home is a hotbed of media interest. We can guess that, when faced with extreme nausea, you want to be away from all of that.

And we can safely deduce that you also want to be with loved ones. Where are most wives likely to head in those circumstances? To their mum, this is where Kate stayed.

Returning to the article, it ends by asking the readers to offer their views as to whether the marriage is on the rocks.

It is a strange society where the uninformed opinions of those unrelated to the topic form the basis of what makes news.

The article in questions was followed, a short while later, by another piece which stated that social media was buzzing with the news that the couple were going to get divorced.

Well, it must be true then.

Another story claims that the Queen has forced the couple apart, calling them work shy and insisting on greater commitment to royal duties.

Ummm. A likely series of events.

When it was announced that her son, Charles, and Princess Diana were separating, she was so upset (even though she knew the announcement was coming) that she took her corgis for a walk.

She returned to Sandringham, where she was staying at the time, turned around and took them out again for another long stroll.

She then repeated the activity. Such was her upset that she needed to be alone to get her head around the announcement. Lucky corgis.

We do know that William and Kate had some breaks during their courtship. As we saw earlier, these were in the lead up to their finals at University, then when William was away with army duties.

In both cases, they found that they wanted to be together again.

Of course, there may have been problems earlier in their marriage. There may be problems today. One day, we might find out from a reliable source.

We did with Charles and Diana, when Diana revealed the truth firstly to the author

Andrew Morton and later in a BBC
documentary.

But, even more probably, their marriage is
strong.

And if it is not, is it really any of our
business?

Doing Her Duty - and more

In line with other royals, Kate is patron and supporter of many charities. Her association with Heads Up, the mental health support organization, is one of her newer ones.

William and Harry are also involved. Their personal experiences of bereavement and the associated mental health concerns following their mother's death provoking such commitment.

Another organization which is particularly dear to Kate is Beatbullying. She suffered herself as a young teen, and now seeks to do all she can to help others in this very difficult position.

Since the birth of her children, she has also become an active advocate of opposition to cyber bullying.

She and her husband met with heads of Facebook and Twitter to discuss ways in which this insidious behavior can be tackled.

One of the unique horrors of cyber bullying is that it is ubiquitous. Like it or not, young people are hooked onto social media, chat rooms and the like.

A bully can exploit this by sending a message at any time. The impact of the fear of the ping on a victim's phone or laptop has led, in severe cases, to suicide.

Bereavement as a child is, naturally, a cause close to William's heart. He is patron of Child Bereavement UK, and Kate supports him actively in his work.

She has talked with and offered sympathy to both adult members who have lost their own children, and youngsters who are suffering bereavement.

She is also a patron of EACH (East Anglia's Children's Hospices). Kate and William lived in Norfolk before returning to London, and the region is close to her heart.

With EACH, she visits and supports children directly as they face their final days.

Two other of the many charities she supports reflect her own love of art. She is patron of the National Portrait Gallery and Art Room.

The latter combines her desire to support those who are most vulnerable with her passion for art. The charity seeks to address issues around self-esteem and teaches life skills to vulnerable children.

It looks to use the power of art to make children more confident and better able to fit into their world. Art Room works with kids who have become disengaged, often excluded, from school.

Indeed, her willingness to give her time to the most vulnerable, and therefore most neglected, members of society is one of her strengths.

She is patron to Action on Addiction. This charity works with drug and alcohol dependents, working to help them to break free from their condition.

Increasingly, with the seemingly unregulated (to any significant degree) rise of online gambling sites, the charity also seeks to support those caught up in this destructive problem.

She is also a supporter of M-PACT, which is unique in being an organization that works with the families of alcohol and substance abusers, seeking to bring them together.

Amongst the numerous other charities which have her patronage, large and small, are The Anna Freud Centre, the 1851 Trust, Action for Children and Sportsaid.

When it comes to charity work, Kate certainly pulls her weight.

Despite the movements forward it has made in the last twenty to thirty years, and these have been considerable, the monarchy remains a somewhat staid and pompous institution.

That is not to suggest that the family is like this. And in all likelihood some of the officials associated with the running of the Palace are not complete fuddy duddies.

(It must be remembered that it was not that long ago that Andrew Morton's book about Diana, written with her direct input, led to the kind of reactionary response that ought to make people laugh.

Amongst other claims and accusations, Morton was called a traitor, and told that he should be imprisoned in the Tower of London.)

But perhaps it is one of the joys of the monarchy that it does still employ outdated and over grand pretensions. This is, after all, what attracts the tourists.

It is also what makes many of the public love the royals, turning out days in advance and sleeping rough to catch a passing glimpse of a waving hand or wonderful hat at a special occasion.

Sometimes it goes too far. Racegoers at Ascot were warned by security men if they got their mobiles out in the Winners' Enclosure after one of the Queen's horses was victorious.

It was not so much the actuality of the warnings – few would argue that the Queen should not enjoy her moment, more the way it was reported.

With astonishingly outdated pomposity, the BBC descended back into the years of subservience, noting that the crowd were giving a 'knowing touch on the arm' if their phone appeared.

'Commoners – know your place.'

But for a modern royal like Kate it is hard to know whether she is proud, amused, bemused or embarrassed by some of the trappings that come with joining the royal family.

It is probably a mixture of all.

She is, of course, a duchess. Some claim that she would rather have been a princess, but to most of us, the title Duchess of Cambridge is fine. Let's not forget that she will become Queen when William accedes to the throne.

She has received the Queen Elizabeth Diamond Jubilee Medal and the interestingly named Tuvalu Order of Merit. This is, as we all know, the highest award of the tiny nation.

One would have thought that just the pleasure of visiting the tiny Commonwealth Island, which is a gem of the Pacific, would be enough. Still, you can't say no.

Kate is also a Canadian Ranger and, perhaps thanks to her parents' work with on commercial aircraft, an Air Commandant of the Air Training Corps (Honorary).

This award, though, might not have been thought through – it is hoped that it doesn't lead to arguments over who would fly the royal chopper.

One of the perks of being a royal, which they certainly couldn't manage without, is the award of a Coat of Arms.

Kate has two, a personal and a married one. The personal Coat hawks back to days gone by, impaling that of her father with the Coat of her husband.

In fact, Michael Middleton and Prince William get on well, there is no impaling involved, metaphorical of otherwise.

Kate also has her Conjugal Coat of Arms, which is not as libidinous as it sounds. It actually features just the couple's individual arms side by side.

As significant today as those duties sanctioned by the Palace, are the informal ones that people expect.

Kate is seen as a fashion icon, and is criticized if she does not live up to this. We know from her time in Anglesey that she likes nothing more than to dress down.

But when out and about on engagements, public of private, the expectation is that she will be dressed to kill.

As much as this might have caused tensions with the palace, it is what her public expect.

Her dress sense is recognized through numerous awards.

She has been awarded 'Best Newcomer' (a while ago now) by the Telegraph and has appeared twice in People Magazine.

Vanity Fair, Style.com and Buzzword have all featured her and she was on the cover of Vogue's centenary issue.

The Tatler placed her eighth in its top ten lists, which probably says more about the magazine than the Duchess.

Mind you, she wasn't a Duchess when Tatler made its call – the title would have been worth a place or two.

Her profile has been maintained by popular culture although, as we have seen, not always in the fairest or most positive way.

William and Kate were the subjects of a 'factionalized' American TV film called, with startling originality, William and Kate.

Mind you, Americans have a record when it comes to dumbing down the titles of films about the royals.

The story goes that when Alan Bennett's stage plays, The Madness of George III, was to be turned into a film, much consternation was caused over the title.

Producers were terrified that audiences would not attend, as they hadn't seen the prequels, The Madness of George I and II.

Whether this is true is a matter of opinion. It would be great if it was. Whatever, the film was released under the title 'The Madness of King George'.

Catching on to the marketing opportunities of a film about the couple, another was made – this time named William and Catherine: A Royal Romance.

Several documentaries have been made about her as an individual and her relationship with William.

But, Kate would have known that she had made it as a popular icon when the results of a survey were published in 2014.

Young adults from overseas were asked to name the people they most associated with UK culture.

Shakespeare, The Beatles, JK Rowling, David Beckham and, along with the Queen, Kate Middleton.

Looking Forward

Kate Middleton came from a wealthy and privileged background, with committed (some might unfairly conclude pushy) parents and a quiet strength of character.

But she is not a blue blood. Whilst this does not make her unique it is unusual for those joining the inner circle of the royal family.

What she has brought, along with her husband and his brother, is a desire to modernize the monarchy.

In many ways, it is easier for Harry and William to achieve this; they have after all, a direct blood line to the House of Windsor.

But the public possesses a fascination with the wives of future kings, and Kate has tried to use that to do good and to bring about change.

At the same time, she also wants to be a mum, and have her own life.

They are not unreasonable ambitions.

Humans are flawed, and that includes the rich and the royals.

In days gone not too distantly by, people were meant to bow before the Heads of State, to doff their hats and be subservient.

The palace guarded every piece of news as though it were the crown jewels, to be closely watched and let out only in protected glimpses.

In those days, the royal family still committed indiscretions. There was still infidelity, and more. It is just that, apart from the most serious happenings, such as the Wallace Simpson affair, nobody knew.

But, for good or bad, today is different. We are all photographers and film makers, able to capture every moment of any incident on our mobiles.

News sources are immense, not just the national papers and television. But those agencies now compete with the spread of online sources, and that has made them, like a hungry lion, merciless.

In those circumstances, somebody in the public eye has such limited privacy. That extends to her family as well.

And, let's be honest, some of the less responsible media outlets, in the absence of anything newsworthy, just make it up.

Those are the conditions that Kate Middleton lives in. Many will say that she made that choice, and it is right, she did.

But why shouldn't she? We don't ask to fall in love.

Time will tell whether William and Kate go on to become King and Queen, or whether there is some truth about the state of their marriage in the unsubstantiated gossip.

Time will tell how many children she has, and how they grow up. Will little George become king? Many of us, though, will probably not live to see that day.

Time will tell the legacy Kate establishes.

But for now, it would be good to let the mother of two young children, who gives much to the nation already, have a bit of space and privacy.

Made in the USA
Columbia, SC
19 June 2019